Why You Are Addicted To Technology

And how to fix the ethical issues
that make us suffer

J.H. Pii

CONTENTS

Introduction   1

1   Analogue Rules to Regulate A Digital World   8

2   Operating as A State Within A State   19

3   Modern Day Aristocratic Anarchy   26

4   From Poisoning the Well to Owning It   36

5   The Elephant in Your Room Made of Your Data   43

6   An Enlightened and Informed Public   61

Sources and Acknowledgements   71

About the Author   82

INTRODUCTION

Thank you for choosing to listen or read to this book. It is an honour I do not take lightly.

I imagine that you are here because you are interested both in new technologies, the platforms you use, how they affect you and what to do about it. Or, it could be that you just saw the Social Dilemma documentary on Netflix, which is as ironic as it is alarming in of itself and you wanted to delve a bit deeper and somehow landed on this book. In any case, as I said, I'm honoured.

Originally this was part of another book I wrote detailing what the platform business model is and the beginner's guide to it. So, more of a managerial and business strategy book. But in sending my mental cleaning-crew to look over my first draft and rewrite sentences, grammatical corrections, and the like. I thought that it would make more sense to have this as separate work on in its own. Partly because I don't think it is the same audience for the two books, although obviously there is some overlap. But also, with the other book there was an inherent disconnect in reading four chapters on how the platform business model works, to then go into all the things wrong or threatening with it at the end. It didn't really make much sense.

But by no means if you think the managerial side of platforms are interesting, or you find yourself being a business owner and/or manager, the other book that I wrote is called, "A Beginners Guide to the Platform Business Model".

Scarface had two rules within the drug dealing business. One, don't underestimate the other guy's greed, and two, don't get high on your own supply. Founders, developers, and CEO's of the large technology companies have been known to not let their kids use technology platforms themselves. Steve Jobs and his kids never used an iPad.* Chris Anderson, former editor of Wired magazine, has strict restrictions on technology-use in his home. Mark Zuckerberg does not use Facebook like you or me, he has twelve moderators to filter his content and employees to help him write his posts. Resembling that of a Public Relations channel for a president elect. Even Apple's Tim Cook told The Guardian, "I don't have a kid, but I have a nephew that I put some boundaries on. There are some things that I won't allow. I don't want them on a social network."*

So, it seems that the creators and founders of these platforms limit or outright bans the use of them. They don't get high on their own supply.

I see platforms, and namely the big technology platforms, as alarming in their conduct and influence, not just over our lives, but also our systems we have built for over thousands of years. In many parts I see the link between platforms conducts and effects to the issues we have today in our societies of sense-making, the news media, social interactions, and the political climate. While many singular examples and problems have been pointed out, it seems to only put focus on the symptoms, not the actual disease – the underlying issue. This book attempts to do just that – that the disease is not the Data Privacy breaches carried out in mass, it is not the endless scroll mechanics specifically made to waste as much time as possible. It is the engine behind it – its business model, and even more zoomed in, the Dataminer category of the platform business model. This is what this book is about, the problems with it, while also suggesting some solutions.

Before we go into the different chapters and what to expect, it is helpful to explain briefly what is meant when I say the Dataminer category, when talking about platforms. This will be a quick overview, where an exhaustively in-depth look can be found in the other business book mentioned earlier. Within platforms out there, we have three overarching categories, or rather two different ones, and one that combines the two.

The first is the Dataminer category. The easiest identifier in this one is in its name, a platform focused on making money from data and advertising exposure, which in relation is your time spent on that platform. The quickest way to spot these platforms is to look at your bank account when using them; if they are free, it is a Dataminer. Examples of these are Facebook, Instagram, Google, TikTok, and Twitter.

Then we have the second one, the Payupper. This category is based on actual transactions being made inside the platforms themselves. If you use these platforms and you see red numbers on your bank account, then that platform is a Payupper. They essentially generate cash flows from money exchanged, rather than on your data itself and advertising exposure. Although they do data-mine to some extent. Examples of these are Uber, Netflix, and JustEast.

When we then combine the two. We get one that initially starts out in having a lite version of that platform, one with ads and data acquisition. But have the option for you to go premium with monthly payments. These platforms are the Frankensteiners. Examples of these are Amazon with Amazon Prime, Spotify, with Spotify Premium, and YouTube with YouTube Premium.*

Now that you know the basics of what the three categories are, know that the main perpetrator is the Dataminer category on what you are about to embark on. This journey is divided into six chapters.

Chapter one shines a light on the outdatedness of our legal system and the slow-to-react governmental institutions to tackle the big Dataminer platform problem. It goes into the fundamental issues that is hard to regulate due to how the free-market and privatising system were developed and goes into the complications happening when a platform becomes too big. You'll be introduced to the Privacy Paradox and Adhesion Contracts, while we delve a bit into the behavioural sciences to tip our toe into what these platforms are psychologically doing to us as well.

Chapter two lays out a historical example of the Dutch East India Company – of what happens when a corporate entity grows too big internationally and links this concern with the giant technology platforms such as Google, Facebook, and Amazon.

Chapter three is a continuation of chapter two, but homes in on the big platforms and their actions related to them monopolising, their "Too Big to Fail" concept, and their unethical behaviour, exemplifying a Facebook Mood Contagion practise. While etching out the United States governments and European Parliament's actions against this. Additionally, you will be explained how the big platforms hijacks as much attention from you as possible through what is known as A/B Testing.

Chapter four goes a bit broader than just the platform and looks at big multinational enterprises in general, to then explain how these went from a more reactive ethical approach, called Corporate Social Responsibility, to a more active one called Creating Shared Value. The businesses motivations behind this change and the actual dangers behind a more active strategy, such as Creating Shared Value, you will get in chapter four.

Chapter five is the big one and finally tackles the meat on the bone. The thing you have thought about up until this very moment and that is data's role for platforms in general, although especially the Dataminer category. This chapter delves head into the waters of Data Privacy and Data Ethics. We will cover the Harm Principle, the Patriot Act, Kant's Humanity Formulation, Foucault's Panopticon, Surveillance Capitalism, the basic links with old school Capitalism itself, the concept of the Admittance of Ignorance, and specific examples seen that platforms have carried or carry out. We get to the root of the problem and the questions we need to answer to fix the problems with the Dataminer platforms, such as Facebook and Twitter. But also playing out the Devil's advocate and looks at the business's perspectives. At the end of this chapter you will get a direct solution to these problems of today. In one sentence and in my opinion, if there is only one chapter you can read or listen to, you should listen to or read this one.

At last we have chapter six. Being the last we look to end the book with a bang. Here the focus is on how the media based Dataminer platforms, such as Facebook, are eroding our democracies and societies from within, but also how the old, more centralised media, is no peach in this matter either. Basically, the very real consequences both on a person-toperson level with our social interactions. But also larger how it breaks our nations if we don't do something about this.

At last, a disclosure is in order. No matter who is writing a book, making a movie, painting, well a painting, or any craft from the corners of the mind. That mind is succumbed to a healthy dose of present fallacy. During the time you create a work, that time is going to affect you and in turn affect the work. I have a grudge against basic education not teaching fallacies and biases, or for that matter, how to change a tire or do your taxes. But at least a list of important fallacies and psychological biases is going to be a book for another time, likely not a tire-changing book.

This ethics book would look very different if it was written back in 2009 where Facebook still was in its infancy and Google were starting to gain market dominance in the areas of search. Google just then began to advance their search algorithms linking it with triangulation and location-based searches, affecting the results based on where you are physically. Just from this some ethical thoughts can be written out, but we are getting a wee bit ahead of ourselves.

Google only laid the groundwork for the far-reaching arm of their data probing practises reaching around you. The same can be said if this book was written in 2029. Who knows how the world would look like at that point, if it would be a dystopian fiction like Bladerunner? Or a liveable haven? I am no futurist, especially not a pessimistic one, either you predict a future people hate and they recent you for it, or it is wrong, and people have forgotten about you, because you were wrong. But the point stands that if this book was written in another timeframe, the ethical perspective on platforms would be severely different. This is not to say that it should not be taken seriously, all works are biased, just that it is useful to know the bias beforehand.

So, my bias is being very critical of Capitalism going rampant, also known as late-stage Capitalism, and critical of the big technology platforms increasingly probing practises. I am by no means anti-Capitalist, not even close, my major is in business. I am in favour of a system that takes advantage of our lizard brain and selfish natures, it brings much innovation and higher standards of living. Just that too much of one thing is unwise. Too much towards one side is bad. A healthy balance needs to be struck. In knowing my bias, I purposely try to take the perspective of both sides and play the Devil's advocate. Which in my opinion have given it a stronger result – I will let you be the judge.

1 ANALOGUE RULES TO REGULATE A DIGITAL WORLD

The problem that has been found with platforms are the antitrust, monopolising, and colluding cases based on outdated regulations. Or rather, the tendencies within the law have tilted towards the businesses favour, over a long process of slow change from consumer to corporate. In metaphorical speak, the frog jumps out of the boiling water if dropped into it – but if submerged into lukewarm water, that is then slowly heated up, the frog boils together with the water.

Predominantly the law regulates based on one-sided, more traditional markets. Not the complex digital platform marketplaces of today. Because the platforms enable businesses to operate within privately-owned spheres, rather than a large public one.* As is the case with much of the law, it is slow and creeping behind the more fast-paced, innovation-driven world of business – especially, the technology industry.

The law and regulations that are set in place aims to promote competition and a free-market economy. But is not geared towards businesses operating and owning their own market environment, within their own private infrastructure.

The issue, therefore, lies in the special conditions and collaborations between the Platformowner, Facebook and Google, and some producing entities within the platform, you and me, or independent companies. Conditions that promotes certain producers' products over others. Conditions such as better discoverability, lower costs, or special services offered, like free shipping or sharing of People Data; your data. Issues also lie in that the Platformowner's own products and services are being marketed on the same platform as the enabled producing entities, as is the case with Netflix. Creating competition between the producing side against the Platform-owner's own offerings. Effectively making it difficult for the Platform-owner not to prioritise their own product line-up over the enabled producing entities. All these complications create a cannibalism-effect for products on the platform between the owner and the enabled producers – they basically eat each other's sales, and a dichotomy is between them.*

For example, there is a strenuous relationship between producers on Netflix, after Netflix decided to introduce more original content in the form of Netflix Originals. Consumers that watch the new episode of The Big Bang Theory does not watch Stranger Things, and vice versa. Even though it is on the same platform, attention given, is attention given away; it's a zero-sum game.

Another example is Amazon's forcing out of certain sellers on their platform, back when onus was on book sales, Amazon forced out independent book retailers, and branding some offerings "Amazon Choice" moving it to the top in consumers search results. All business decisions that creates an unfair market environment within their own private platform but resembling a marketplace the size of countries. In any case, many of the big platform's conducts and their allegedly ethically grey or outright bad behaviour will be laid out littered throughout this book, with many more examples to boot.

To explain the problem in simpler prose. Imagine if your government ventured into all the industries you see around today. Products and services you used to see from private entities, are now public. These public offerings give themselves unfair advantage opposed to the private ones, because the public owns the market setting itself, so why not, legally they can. The governmental offerings do not have Value Added Taxes and in effect have a lower price-tag or impossible requirements of standards are placed on the private offerings. All the while a select few private products and services have had delightful dinners with the public market owner and got granted lower cost conditions to artificially increase their profit margins. Does not seem like a fair and free market does it?

To cover another example that shines a light on the growing problem and is indicative on the recent developments within business practises and the law. We have the emergence of Adhesion Contracts.

We are going to cover data rights and privacy in a later chapter in this book. But for now, in covering Adhesion Contracts, there is large overlap in the waving of rights from consumers, being inadvertently forced to give consent to something adverse towards them, to the stands against data rights and privacy. That consumers have to willingly act against their own selfinterest. This one-sided practise where the business gets the better end of the deal and where no meeting of minds exist, between the consumer and business, is known as Adhesion Contracts.*

When you sign up for a digital service, let's say Google Mail; you create your email, type in your information and get prompted to read a lengthy document stating all the legalities you have to accept. All the rights you have to waver away, otherwise no Google Mail. I personally do not know any who reads this lengthy document – Google knows this, so they decided recently to sum it up after you click the "agree button" in an abbreviated box. This is likely a development due to the growing distrust and scepticism there is against technology giants, like Google today. Just look at the writing of this book. But I digress.

The point of this, is that consumers essentially do not have a choice. Since if they do not agree to the text no one reads, they do not get Google Mail. Yes, there do exist other email services out there, but when you are the size of Google, then it poses a problem. Because what about Google Maps? Or Google Search? How about your Android smartphone?

Even circumstances, let's say a new job, who requires you to develop a Google Mail make you have even less of a choice. I have heard people argue that no one forces people to sign up for Google's services or the like. If you want, you can choose to live in a tent out in the woods and discover your inner hunter-gatherer. We live in a free world, no one is stopping you from tent-living. It should be pretty obvious that this is not a viable argument for a myriad of reasons; some being social exclusion, inefficiency in living, and so on and so forth.

Legally this issue, as previously mentioned, is known as "Adhesion Contracts". Contracts that are drafted up by only one party, Google, in which the other side, you, has no say or changes on the matter. The problem with this is that privacy agreements are these adhesion contracts. No matter if an abbreviated box pops up or not. Since you as the other party has no say in these contracts and is not a 'meeting of minds' as it is supposed to be.

Over the span of decades these adhesion contracts have been more of a development and recognised in the court of law and it is hurting our society in the way that it maximises the power of businesses today, away from consumers and people; you and me. A recent and more personal example was after I bought a Microsoft Surface, super amp to set it up, I naturally sat it up. When the adhesion contract popped up it even cheekily said that I could choose not to agree, but that would mean no Microsoft Surface, I guess I had to refund it then. Although few stores would accept this Adhesion Contract argument as a valid refund reason.

Related to this, is the conundrum of the age-old thought experiment within philosophy called 'the Prisoners Dilemma'. This experiment is mirroring why consumers today actively, and in some cases knowingly, act against their own self-interest.*

The Prisoner's Dilemma goes like this.

You and your partner-in-crime sit nervously inside your poorly airconditioned Honda Civic. The Honda was specifically chosen to be dark purple and a little bit dusty – to avoid prying eyes, you both agreed. You both do not really like each other. But your likeness of bank notes exceeds your disliking of the other. You go over the plan once again, each a bit annoyed of why you have to go over everything a fifth time, but you both power through. You rush into the local town's bank to get the money.

It could be because neither of you were listening to the other, again because of the disliking, or that you wanted the better end of the deal. Needless to say, coordination between you was horrible and you got tackled by the police on the way out.

Now, you find yourself separate and alone inside a grey, depressing room, with one mirrorwindow, one camera, microphone, and a cop named Joe sitting down with a Styrofoam cup of Joe. The coffee-cop gives you two options; stay silent or confess. If you confess and your annoying partner stays silent, he gets ten years behind metal bars and you walk free. But if both of you confess, then you get early parole, and both get five years. And if both of you trusts each other, and stays silent, you both get three years. The dilemma and why it got its name, "The Prisoners Dilemma", is that objectively it is better if both of you confesses, in hopes of walking free. But since both know this, both will confess, and the outcome of both of you is worse. You, therefore, should have stayed silent to get the minimum sentence for you both. It is essentially a question between individual and group rationality.

The problem with this Privacy Paradox is that it seems that privacy is at the onus of the individual to choose to opt in or opt out of services that probes you for data. This makes sense in many western individualistic and humanitarian societies, where focus is on the individual to choose how they live. But this discount the groups rationality of choosing to opt in, which generate enough mass for the individual to not being able to opt out. Resulting in the individual begrudgingly chooses an option against their own self-interest. Which means that multiple individuals does this – the multiple individuals choosing to opt in becomes the group, which entices other individuals, and the circle of privacy degradation has begun.

Now this is the philosophical and sociological viewpoint explaining the phenomenon of the Privacy Paradox. The psychological finding that have been postulated over a number of years, backed by scientific research, and aggregated by Susanne Barth and Menno de Jong back in 2017, is that while the individual believes to be concerned about privacy and wants higher control over the disclosure of their activities. They do an internal risk-benefit analysis and deems the risk to be none or slim, compared to the proposed benefits.*

While the truth, in most cases, lies somewhere in the middle. Yes, the individual, you and me, carry out quickly, inside of our minds, either consciously or unconsciously, if we should sign up for a service and how much information to give to that service to be worth the supposed benefit, linked with the possible risks and your own idealistic viewpoint on privacy. But in most cases this a quick decision, at least taking my example and I know a bunch of other people who also sign up without much rationale and careful thought. Granted it only is the case with a digital service that is well known, like Facebook, Google, and Amazon. Whereas the opposite is the case with smaller, more unknown platforms. The reason why I point this out is that within decision-making, discovered by Daniel Kahneman and Amos Tversky*, is that you can decide something in a quick, off-hand manner, your Fast Brain, largely running unconsciously. For example, what is $2 + 2$? What is the capital of Germany? A well-groomed man with a designer suit, Rolex watch, and an approachable smile, suddenly shows that he has gang-tattoos and scar tissue all over the backside of his body. You answer these questions quickly without any afterthought and you react quickly to something unexpected related to preconceptions. The decision to sign up for larger, marketleading platforms, is carried out largely by your Fast-Thinking brain. Oppositely, you have the slow and rational brain. This kicks in when you are at a Math exam and you consciously devote focused attention towards problems, questions and situations. For example, what is 2 * 87 / 45? This Slow Brain takes up more energy and was developed during the time where we had to conserve energy, because food was scarce, we were Hunter-Gatherers with a lazy brain opting more times than not for the Fast-Thinking one.

In general, if we all could only make decisions based on our Slow Brain we would make much more calculated and rational choices and is where Stoicism comes in. But we are veering away from the topic at hand and I can write reems of words about behavioural decision-making and psychological effects, of which I likely will, but not now in this book. Just consider that the risk-benefit analysis you carry out in big well-known platforms is done without much afterthought and the opposite is the case for smaller, up-and-coming platforms. A big discrepancy that feeds into the already difficult terrain of going up against the monopolising giants of Facebook, Google, and Amazon.

Combining this with the individual choice colliding with the group choice to then affect the individual choice, and the risk-benefit analysis linked to this equation, is almost in a way predetermined before you even open the Gmail website or smartphone application.

This we will delve into in more detail in chapter five, when we deep-dive into the black pools of data rights and the enabling factor that data is directly linked to the success of platforms, especially the Dataminer version.

The next large issue in the developments of the platform ethically is known as "nonownership ownership".* This, again, delves into the areas of Behavioural Economics and the psychological ownership, or Endowment Effect, that a consumer feels when owning or having access to a product. Again, a whole book can be written about these psychological effects. But for now, this ownership effect means that you value a product more when you have acquired it in some way, or you feel a kinship with the product in whatever manner. Basically, you value a cup more if it has your name on it, compared to a cup without your name on it. So, the coffee-cup named Joe, would value his Joe-cup more than just a random Styrofoam cup. You superimpose your identity into the products and services you own.

This is the case even if you are subscribing to a pool of rotating products, rather than buying them. You feel an ownership towards temporary products that you subscribe to. Giving you the feeling of ownership, without actually having legal ownership.* While this attachment of one's identity into the products we buy or subscribe to is a scale, a gradient. Sara Dommer and Vanitha Swaminathan found out in 2013* that if there is an existential threat against you, either environmentally through a president that got elected that you don't agree with, or that a pandemic has locked-down the whole world so you cannot see anyone, or internally through a break-up, or a loss of a job or a family member, makes your sense of ownership into these items you own stronger. This is explained in that your ego artificially increase the sense of value towards your products, to inadvertently increase your own sense of identity, to keep you afloat and ignore these crises against your sense of identity.

While it should be noted that Dommer and

Swaminathan also discovered that this sense of self into one's products and services also work in the development of your social identity – meaning your sense of you connected to a group.

Ergo when you combine on Dataminer social platforms like Instagram, Twitter, and Facebook, both literally your conscious behaviour and data, connected with groups, and figuratively, through the mere ownership effect for all products and subsequent brands, Android over Apple, PlayStation over Xbox over Nintendo. Then that means your sense of identity into a digital self, means you multiply your sense of ownership towards these platforms and artificially makes you value these Dataminer platforms even higher. Becoming nigh addicted – making in turn the Dataminer platforms profit from this effect.

Within the media platform model, a central practise is on an ever-changing selection of products, which the consumer is then subscribed to. This means that legally the consumer holds no rights over these products, and no accountability can be put on the media corporations themselves, having effectively detached the liabilities it would normally have without losing the psychological ownership that you have.

It should be said that this framing is rather one-sided. Since upsides, such as more products can be introduced, and lesser known products can find its audience, is enabled through this rotating product concept. It essentially increases the likelihood that smaller producers and niche products can be introduced, making the overall market a richer environment. This was seen in the rise of the smaller, more independent movie and music scene due to Netflix's and Spotify's lower barriers of entry and rotating selection of products. If a product failed, it would only fail temporarily and the cost of hosting that digital product was slim. While these smaller creators could find its niche audience due to this large consumer pool. This effectively increases innovation within an industry, because more rapid testing of new product ideas can be tried due to this larger potential marketplace.

2 OPERATING AS A STATE WITHIN A STATE

The problem still stands that Big Business do not have a Business Philosophy, or rather their philosophy is based on the shareholder movement of growth and profit, not moral and altruistic good. Businesses do not have an ethical guideline, which is concerning when you start to consider the influence that Big Business has on you, me, and our whole societies. See one tracks everything you purchase; another is tracking everyone you interact with and what your interests are, another is tracking all your movements and all your actions through your online behaviour – I can keep going. In multiple databanks there are thorough profiles about you, who you are, your interests. These technology giants likely know more about you than you know about yourself. This is a problem when the biggest marketplace in the world, Amazon, is a company separate from a governmentally managed public marketplace. Achieving a valuation higher than Colombia, Uruguay, Paraguay, Bolivia, Peru, Ecuador, Venezuela, Guyana, and Suriname combined, based on all these countries Gross Domestic Product. A concept referred to as, "Too Big to Fail".

Although, and rather ironically, this goes against the theory laid out in the more business management(ey) focused book on the platform model, I also have written. More detail can be found in that book, titled, "A Beginners Guide to the Platform Business Model". But briefly here, it is concerning that if a platform organically or strategically grows to such a size, that for example YouTube has, that it then becomes too big to manage successfully. YouTube and other platforms of such a size has to revert back to automated systems, algorithms, and bureaucracy to manage their platform, to their own great detriment. YouTube's producing side, its private video creators – you and me – are fed up with all the complications that YouTube has introduced. Multiple examples can be written, but a big one is the Copy Rights, Fair Use, and flagging issue, colliding with the removal of revenue on videos, even channels being outright banned.

When we take a look at the annals of history and the dangers of Too Big to Fail, a multitude of companies spring forth. But since this is not a history book, we will only look at the United East India Company, or, as is more commonly known: the Dutch East India Company. The main point of taking a few glances at this early modern-age trading company, is to learn of a scenario likely to happen if the big technology platforms of today are not regulated or broken up.

The Dutch East India Company was the first joint-stock trading company and was respectively named; Vereenigde Oostindische Compagnie, or simpler, VOC. We will look at their direct influence through their Foreign Direct Investments and their use of monopolisation,

Colonialism, exploitation, slave trade, and use of violence. All to achieve the status as the most powerful company in history, based on the time they were in.*

The VOC was a trade conglomerate banded together from many rival trading companies in the Netherlands. It got together to form and operate as the first publicly traded joint-stock company in history. Combining this with a newly established building called; Beurs van Hendrick de Keyser. Which, incidentally, also was the first stock exchange in history. So, the stock exchanges and publicly traded companies we have today, was invented by the Dutch.*

At the Keyser investors both from the Netherlands and abroad could invest in the VOC and subsequently their trading operations abroad to profit from. But as it was stipulated, investors only owned a small share on the goods being traded on a shipping vessel. Back then the practise of mercantilism and foreign-shore trading was an extremely dangerous and volatile endeavour. So, the Netherlands did the third ingenious invention; a trustworthy legal system.*

See the investors was secured by a separate court system, detached from the national monarchy. A legal structure unprecedented back in the 1600s and inspired trust to invest your excess coins into the VOC. The trust came from a judicial system, since a legal system based on a monarch were liable to corruption in conjunction to the personality of the king or queen, and is incidentally why the International Criminal Court today is situated in The Hague – giving a nod to the Dutch inventiveness in legal proceedings.*

The VOC, due to the Dutch war of liberation from the Spanish empire, was granted monopoly status in its first

21-year period to fuel the Dutch economy and military might. Practically, the VOC was managed by a 17-member board named "the Heeren Zeventeen". The historian Stephen Bown in his book 'Merchant Kings: When Companies Ruled the World' described this monopoly status as, "the VOC would essentially operate as a state within a state."*

The VOC mainly had dealings in the Southeast Asian countries, chief among them, Indonesia. Within this area the VOC sat up forts and other mercantile structures and supply chains. All to control trade and product flow in this central trading area. The VOC gained more and more power in the name of profit and control over supply lines from these Foreign Direct Investments, operating on profit margins peaking at around 1500 percent. While combining this with their increasing military might, boasting at its peak at 40 war vessels and 150 cargo ships. The VOC was a force to behold fuelled by wealthy, everyday Europeans, with money to spare.*

The VOC's monopoly status of 'its own state within a state' enabled them to wage war, imprison and execute convicts, negotiate treaties, print its own currency, and set up permanent establishments. Needless to say, the VOC if translating their influence in today's world would land at around, and adjusting for inflation, at 8.4 trillion US dollars here in 2021 today.* More valuable than every country today, outside of the United States and China.

Humans are notorious for being awful at conceptualising big numbers so, let us keep ourselves in this rabbit hole and see what those trading company Dutchies could pay for today. The Dutch East India Company could fully purchase companies that have widespanning effects on all our lives, many of them centred around in this very book. They could acquire Walmart, Amazon, Apple, Alphabet, or Google, Facebook, Microsoft, Twitter, General Motors, Coca-Cola, Disney, Nike, Ikea, and General Electric, with money to spare.

In the public sector, just to see what public benefits the VOC could subsidise today for all our benefit would be paying all American elementary school teacher's salary for eighty years.* If we stay within the educational sector, this trading company could effectively make a private four-year college degree free of charge for twelve years.* That is a lot of blue cup/red cup youngsters and books.

Just to name a few interesting facts; Cape Town today was founded by the VOC using the place as a pitstop before heading to the east indies, and New Zealand today gets its name from the VOC. While Australia would have been called New Holland, from its original name: Nova Hollandia, if not for the British, later on in history.*

The VOC essentially saw trade routes as their own currency – the more they had control over, the wealthier they would be. They proceeded to monopolise trade in and out of Indonesia, Sri Lanka, and the only Europeans allowed to trade in Japan. While establishing key forts and mercantile structures in the maritime distribution lines from China to India.

How the VOC did this can in large part be contributed to one man named Jan Peiterszoon Coen, who famously said, "Your honours know by experience that trade in Asia must be driven and maintained under the protection and favour of Your Honours' own weapons, and that the weapons must be paid for by the profits from the trade; so that we cannot carry on trade without war nor war without trade."*

And thus, began the interlinking between Capitalisms unrelenting pursuits of profits, and a government aiding it for the cash flows to free and de-seawater a nation – the Netherlands. But at the cost of atrocities and war. To understand Jan Pieterszoon Coen, who believed that establishing a monopoly of trade only could be achieved by expelling and eliminating the local populace. We have to go into one particular moment that might have shaped him.

In 1608 a statement from the 17-member board, back in The Hague, was given, "We ask your attention for the islands where clove and nutmeg grow and we order you to conquer these islands for the VOC, either through negotiation or violence."*

In reaction 300 soldiers were sent to Naira Island to rebuild a fort from Portuguese ruins. The local population and respective figure of the Banda, on Naira Island, only wanted to negotiate with the Dutch if they had a hostage as guarantee. The Dutch agreed and brought with them a British one, who the Netherlands and VOC was at a cold war with. They set a negotiation date, showed up, but they were met with no respective figure, so they looked around.

They eventually found the figure. But the figure was dismayed when they saw the soldiers the VOC had brought to the negotiation tropical table and said to come again, this time with fewer soldiers. The VOC agreed again and did, but it was a trap. The local populace sprang out and slaughtered all of 46 Dutch VOC's, with one person, Jan Pieterszoon Coen, witnessing this horror in full display.* Imagine the hatred he must have gotten from this experience, how jaded he had become. He then proceeded, when Coen got elected Governor General by the 17-member board, to eliminate the Bandanese people in the name of profit and trade control. He did, and went on to Lontor Island, conquering it and establishing permanent presence there. Where Coen imported slaves from all over the region to work on the farms with harsh working conditions and abysmal pay.

So, why are we talking about this old trading company? In a lot of ways if a corporation runs too large, becoming Too Big to Fail, the consequences of this, if it originates from an institution that runs on the business philosophy of profit and Capitalism – an organisation that does not care about human rights, altruism, or ethical standards. Then this power, influence and freedom of design can pose as a huge problem on you and me, our way of life, and our nations.

This very development is starting to happen with the big technology platforms. Just to mention a few examples, Facebook wants to establish their own currency in the form of cryptocurrency, while they at the same time have begun to enable transactions on their platform – it doesn't take much imagination, or slippery slope, to detach the currency from a nations one, to Facebook's own.

But the VOC did not grow to become this big on their own, they had governmental support. They had the backing of operating 'as a state within a state'. We should learn from the VOC's past and not copy the power and influence one corporation can achieve with the approval of governments, not just in the name of competition, but in the name of our established systems and the well-being of you and me.

3 MODERN DAY ARISTOCRATIC ANARCHY

In the words described as early as in 1910 by former president Woodrow Wilson, with the serene New Jersey beaches clashing in the background, he said, we have the ones that must do what they are told, and then we have the few with an imperial freedom of design.* This imperial freedom of design implores the few big Platform-owners to use their private power to influence public-living in ways that resemble the Aristocratic Anarchy of the middle ages.

12th century England was a place of knighthood, manners and nobility. But was also a place of aristocratic influence and power that rivalled each other and feuded, to the extend as to be a feudal anarchy. In some ways, businesses can be seen in their influence, or potential influence, to rival that of this feudal English anarchy. In the sense that they wage conflict only to gain more market control – more profit. This comparison is of course put on the edge. Since in the Middle Ages, war and very real casualties was a thing of daily life. This we do not see today.

But let us say that government X in a multiparty democratic nation suggests increasing taxes by one percent. This would be subject to vigorous debate back and forth. The political value of this, the specifics demanded down to the smallest details of what the extra tax money would be used for. Arguments linked with personal freedom and individuality. Value rebuttals based on equality, not leaving its citizens behind. Who are the taxed and who needs the taxes? Where after months and months of back and forth, it would end up with an increase in taxes of one third of one percent.

If Amazon decided to increase their service cost on all of its products offered, arguing for higher managerial costs, let's say by 10 percent. Then that would happen, no discussion, no major issues. Likewise, if Twitter chooses to ban people, effectively censoring and filtering information and free speech, then they can do this, no discussion, no legal consequences. But if Amazon's marketplace platform resembles that of countries and affects people's lives like how a tax increase would affect people's lives, and if Twitter is so ingrained in the US media and sense-making – then that is something to think about, and maybe should be hold accountable as states and governments are held accountable. Or maybe an alternative variant of this.

But, I hear you say, cannot the producers and consumers of the Amazon platform then not just find another platform? Likewise, why can't the people banned on Twitter not just find another platform? And Amazon and Twitter are held accountable, they are just held accountable by market forces. If Twitter ban enough people, then they don't have customers, and Amazon increasing their prices universally by 10 percent, would lose sales as a result. All good points, but not when that is the only platform out there and not only that, but also if

Amazon controls the means to launch a new platform to begin with – creating a significant lock-in effect and barrier of entry for new platforms. Then that is the danger with monopolistic corporations and the "Too Big to Fail" concept. I go more into detail about this in my previously mentioned, more business-oriented management book.

What this example illustrates is that private business actors, especially within the platform model, operate in a way that would be unthinkable in the public sphere, within the confines of a democratic government.

Platforms have received criticisms of gaining too much market power through colluding with multiple, separate entities, known as anti-trust and mergers. Michael Katz have spent two decades of his life researching and investigating these very issues.* Problems of market riggings by the Platform-owner's own range of products in conflict with the producing thirdparty side. Where the Platform-owner, since it is owned privately, creates favourable conditions for their own products and services as opposed to the third-party competitors. This legally is a grey area, since it is a privately-owned platform but poses complications when it is platforms at the size of countries' economies and the power to shape the citizens view on important political matters inside of nations.

Like Google with its practises of their search engine being the default on the Android operating system. This makes sense since Google owns Android and has Google Chrome as their default browser but is a problem when many other Smartphone hardware manufactures, like Samsung, has to have Google Chrome as default on their phones. It would be equivalent to Microsoft demanding that all computers, desktop, two-in-ones, and laptops has to have the whole Microsoft Office Suite. Although to see it more fairly, smartphones consumers can download another smartphone browser, and on Microsoft, their own browser, Microsoft Edge is the default, many just download Google Chrome or Firefox more readily on computers.

But behind the scenes, reality takes a different perspective. To go back to Google's browser, Chrome, Google pays smartphone manufacturers like Apple vast sums of money to default all search, speech and tapping, to be Google search, connected with Apple's Siri. Google has effectively set up an advertising cash flow loop of gaining advertising from their search engine from Samsung and Apple, to pay Samsung and Apple to default the Google search engine on their smartphones. A perfect example of the platform model enacting ecosystem control, creating innovation influences and cornering of market shares from competitors.

To go a bit more in-depth. The U.S. Justice Department on the 20th of October 2020 filed a lawsuit against Google for these very anti-competitive and anti-trust practises.* Something that historically is nothing new, just ask the tobacco, petrol, and telecommunications industry. The U.S. Justice Department have up until then been criticised in lacking behind the anti-competitive agents of the European Union billing Google upwards of 9 billion US dollars.* While warning to go beyond mere fines if not course-corrected in a timely manner.

A statement by Executive Vice President, Margrethe Vestager, for the European Commission under her tagline; 'A Europe fit for the digital age' said, "the new rules will require digital services, especially the biggest platforms, to be open about the way they shape the digital world that we see. They'll have to report on what they've done to take down illegal material. They'll have to tell us how they decide what information and products to recommend to us, and which ones to hide, and give us the ability to influence those decisions, instead of simply having them made for us. And they'll have to tell us who's paying for the ads that we see, and why we've been targeted by a certain ad."*

The law that the recent U.S. Justice Department lawsuit is being filed under is the almost century old act of the 1890, the Sherman Act. This act stands to go against two aspects; anticompetitive agreements, and unilateral conduct that monopolises, or attempts to monopolise, the relevant market.* Both of which the platform business model specifically aims for, especially the Dataminer category, fuelled by advertising and your data.

See Google, based on the incentive to keep you on Google's services, have made a change over the last ten years of burying search results outside of Google themselves. They essentially in only showing you results from other Google products, or ads which pay Google to show their result. All trying to get you to click on a result that either Google gets paid for per click, or referring you to one of the other many Google services, like YouTube, for you to watch two non-skippable ads, or Google Maps, tracking where you are and selling this data to nearby stores.

This Dataminer business model is designed to make you into the product, you as the means to get advertising money. Their incentive is to keep you engaged and milk as much conscious attention on their services as humanly possible. They achieve this in a rational, mathematical way.

The Adam Alter book, 'Irresistible, the rise of addictive technology and the business of keeping us hooked' lays this out in a neat way. What the Dataminer platforms in particular carries out to keep you engaged, is known as A/B Testing and Optimisation.*

For this to not turn into a business analytics book, is here a more digestible example from Adam Alter himself. While we will highlight a more concrete problem related to this after.

A/B testing is the trial of two scenarios, with one particular purpose in mind. Let's say the goal is to maximise time-spent on platform X, a common goal on the Dataminer category. Let's also say that the platform is a game where you have to complete a quest. In order to complete this quest, you can go through a buzzling city with impressions everywhere, let's call it option A, or, you go through a serene mountain-scape repeatedly capturing awe of the views, this is option B. After some time and the test have run its course on multiple people to track their time-spent on the platform, you see that time-spent, your attention, was maximised with option A: the city tour. So, the platform to complete a quest is now through a city.

Then let's do an A/B testing on what to do in this city? Here we do a test of retrieving an item, in a set of items, a good old treasure hunt, again, option A, or, talking to all the people to investigate a thrilling mystery, option B. You see that talking to people gains the most attention and time-spent, so now your platform-game is in a city, doing an investigation, by talking to people. You repeat this process thousands of times, becoming more and more intricately detailed and you end up with a mathematically enhanced platform in capturing as much as your attention as possible.

The issues with the attention economy, as it is known, is that it is a zero-sum game competing for your brain space. Here is a real-world example from Facebook themselves and then we go into the problems. Facebook found out, through a previous A/B test, that new moms who cooks their own Do-It-Yourself baby food, also had a propensity for being against vaccines. The moms that joined the Facebook group, "DIY Baby Food" therefore got recommended groups such as "the Anti-Vacciners" group. If they then joined this group, then another A/B test showed Facebook that these had a propensity for conspiracy theories, so they got recommended groups such as the Flat-Earthers and QAnon. Now new moms that just wanted to feed their babies healthy home-cooked meals are QAnons and Flat-Earthers.*

It is no coincidence that QAnon and Flat-Earther members spiked during the COVID-19 pandemic lockdown, since people spent significantly more time on Dataminer platforms like Facebook than ever before and got presented time and time again with the dopamine spike every time you see the red icon next to the bell.

Now, by no means is it the only indicator, QAnon for example feeds on distrust in one's system and political leaders, and this distrust grew to enormous amounts during the pandemic. QAnon laid out a backstory, a reason, why X government was so corrupt. It created a monolithic scapegoat of a corrupted, corrupting, and all-powerful world elite as an alternative to break the bleak reality that the pandemic came with. When people feel powerless they revert to extreme beliefs, and QAnon is by all means an extreme belief. It is modern mythmaking, a wandering folktale, and it is highly interesting. It started as scary camp-fire creepypasta-stories online in 2017 and turned through, the coined Cass Sunstein and Timur Kuran term; availability cascades*, in a self-reinforcing cycle evolving inevitably into a movement from 2020/2021 evangelised to this day by what philosopher Henry Lefebvre would call Surrealists people, living in a fantasy, in an escapist world and intermingling this fiction with the real world.* This is likely going to be its own book sometime in the future, who knows.

We will delve into the very real consequences of society degradation and how the technology platforms are at least partly responsible in the last chapter. But for now, in order for a society to function as a democracy, realised by Plato, Aristotle, and Rousseau, you need an enlightened and informed public.* If enough people spiral down into focusing more on Agenda News, such as what Trump tweeted last week or what the newest insight into the mystery of the backdoor Q-people are. Then that removes attention given from Reflective News, such as the deeper issues with late-stage Capitalism, the increasing inequality of wealth based from both capital and labour*, and global warming making us commit a slow world population seppuku.

A rebottle would be that these platforms only recommends content, no one is forcing people to consume it. But this is a limited point of view, which we will delve into a bit deeper in chapter five, about data and data privacy. For now, to not be a full tease, is that recommendations and what you are exposed to shapes your mind. If you only see angry posts on Facebook, then you are a significantly angrier person and in turn posts more angry posts, creating a self-defeating effect for other people exposed to your angry posts.* Likewise, over 70 percent of all videos consumed on YouTube comes from YouTube's recommended videos, based on your watch behaviour and A/B-figured-out what you would be interested in.* And a last point, these groups like QAnon, Antivaccinators, and FlatEathers are an Echo-Chamber in of themselves. Confirming their belief and bias between each other, rather than being challenged and provoking a more critical thinking – which is generally the case with old media, where you can't choose your content, so you are exposed to a myriad of topics. Making you more widely learned and critical.

It should be said that even old media are biased and shaped through outside forces and coercion. The concept of the Mohawk Valley formula developed by philosopher Noam Chomsky speaks directly to this.* The formula is based on that governmental entities and multinational enterprises does not remove the ability to protest, but controls what is being protested through media and propaganda manipulation; of controlling the message. Noam explains this in his own way, when questioned by an honourable journalist being sceptical of if he really was influenced and are self-censoring. Noam responded, "I'm sure you believe everything you're saying. What I'm saying is that if you believed something different you wouldn't be sitting where you're sitting."*

The difference in the Big Tech companies is that these A/B tests are aided by millions of millions of data points, crunched by self-learning algorithms with no ethical standpoint or directions other than making money. Maximising the attention hoarding of the platforms and in effect creates a digital drug. It can be speculated that this is how the Endless Scroll mechanic got epitomised into every platform out there. See you can say that optimising a product based on a goal is no new concept. When a movie director films a movie, they want that movie to be as good as possible. Same with a video games designer for a game and a painter with a painting. But the complication is the sheer size of these A/B tests enabled by massive data sets and complicated algorithms to distil these into actionable choices. The movie, video game and painting does not even come close to these technology companies' actions. Just imagine how much time infinite scrolling in Instagram, Facebook, and Twitter has been wasted for millions of people in the world.

To conclude this attention economy section, it should be mentioned that the larger issue is with the Dataminer platform itself or underlying its business model. There is a reason why Netflix has removed their auto-play mechanic and that TikTok instantly plays a video just when you log-in. The former is a Payupper; the latter is a Dataminer. The former makes its money on direct deposits of money from the consumer, you and me, and the latter makes money on the attention, time, and behaviour spent on the platform, sometimes not even when on the platform itself.

4 FROM POISONING THE WELL TO OWNING IT

Which brings us to the new development within business ethics, conduct and governing of reactionary patchwork toward active good. Businesses today in their responding to increased pressures from employees inside the corporations and educational sectors conditioning the future employees, governmental incentives, and funding, changing media focus and larger culture shaping, and change in consumer spending towards more ethical and sustainable products. All of these parameters have demanded that businesses enact a more ethical conduct. And so, from Corporate Social Responsibility in the past, CSR, came Creating Shared Value now, CSV.

The more reactionary Corporate Social Responsibility is a reactive practise that aims to patchwork the damages already done in the name of monetary growth and a collective 'Hurray!' from shareholders.*

"Oh, we dumped toxic chemicals in the freshwater lake you townsfolk use for clean drinking water. Sorry, but fret not intrepid drinkers. We have Corporate Social Responsibility now to fix it all up by pumping another chemical into the lake to kill the aforementioned toxic chemical to make it clean again. Drink up!"

Social pressure started to catch on and realised that Corporate Social Responsibility was not enough to enact significant change in the damages carried out by Big Business. While the realisation came in large part also from that multinational enterprises have a significant impact on not just a nations society and well-being, but the world, when looking through the lens of the global warming crisis. These businesses started to change and implemented the humanities, namely sociology, anthropology, and philosophy, into their business governance. Figuring out a win-win practise of enacting social and environmental good, while also achieving financial growth. And so, Creating Shared Value was invented.*

Through the change in business mentality is now new developments such as the Circular Economy, following the ReSOLVE strategies of Regenerate, Share, Optimise, Loop, Virtualise, and Exchange*, while durability and lifespans of products where increased either through the same purpose or biodegradability, shepherded through the name of 'cradle to cradle'. While more actionable and holistic business models have come out to focus on these three values of environmental, social and financial, names of business models such as Business Cycle Canvas and Triple Layered Business Model Canvas.* The point being is that things are changing, but these more forward-thinking changes are starting in the educational sector and consumer demand, to coerce businesses to change. I will likely some time in the future write a practical-minded book about this, to promote more actionable good in big business. Something that very well can happen with the big platforms themselves, out there.

Creating Shared Value is rooted in the insight that markets, society, the environment, and businesses are interdependent of each other, or in normal language; they are linked. A market, in essence, is a collection of communities and clusters of micro-groups that have to possess enough disposable income, in order for these communities to be viable markets for said businesses. All the while society and political structures control and steer these markets, hopefully towards the better. So through this, Creating Shared Value came barrowing in and puts an emphasis on socio-economic growth, as part of a business's competitive strategy, within these markets, because these markets are linked with financial performance.*

In some cases, this mentality has even been seen stretched on of which social infrastructure investments from businesses in poorer, third world countries, aims to develop new, future markets for their business. If this gets to be a reality, more than it already is in the form of philanthropy, then this means that businesses in the form that they own their privately-owned markets, through the platform business model, owns public goods such as roads, the fire department and schools. Based on the indirect benefits of creating an efficient market to transport goods on the new roads, protected customers and future employees from not burning to the ground – from the new fire department, while these people are more monied through education from the new schools.

The economists Michael Porter and Mark Kramer who coined the term Creating Shared Value, explains it this way, "... policies and operating practises that enhance the competitiveness of a company while simultaneously advancing the economic and social conditions in the communities in which it operates."*

38

A multi-billion-dollar international enterprise can invest in new and updated schools within a market. Which the government of that market has struggled with in the past. This due to the low tax income from the low education level or high amount of corruption within public institutions in these nations. Also known as the poverty trap. This the business can help with, investing in these schools directly to raise the income level, which as an effect raises their disposable income, making them potential consumers for their own business.

Within international economics this scholarly is known as Foreign Direct Investments and is supported by the theory of 'Trickle-Down Economy'. A theory that has been criticised thoroughly, but has some strong examples which speaks for it, such as South Korea and China. So these private investments aids the country in a myriad of ways. While inadvertently the business will make it known that they have heavily invested in these schools, so the students will have a positive perception of that business. A sort extreme Apple strategy, with Apple targeting students in large part so they prefer Apple when they are educated and ergo keeps buying Apple products when they have more money.

It is, therefore, a change in business mentality from short-term profit making towards longterm value creation, which inevitably leads to profits. A shift from Corporate Social Responsibility, criticized by the famed economist Milton Friedman in 1970, as firms are inherently self-contained entities which are forced to react to negative world consequences from internal favourable business strategies.* Creating Shared Value aims to bridge this gap of business perception with implementing growth parameters and strategy development internally together with environmental and social needs – providing a more permanent good into both the business and society.

This sounds all new and revolutionary, but is actually in line with what Adam Smith in his manifesto 'The Wealth of Nations' based Capitalism on back in 1776.*

Adam argued that if a rich person becomes rich enough to cover the necessary expenses, they will start to consume outside of their necessities. He spoke more in line with the factory owner will invest in his factory to make others rich through hiring new employees. But the other argument of the rich person also holds water, that one rich person makes the other a richer person, and one poor person makes the other a poorer person. Egoism is Altruism. Or in the Wallstreet movies scripts, "Greed is good". Although in late-stage Capitalism this can be taken way too far. But this is for another book.

Creating Shared Value is predicated on the idea of utilising the humanities in developing new markets into making these markets richer for the businesses gain. It is an idealised view of making the world a better place, in the name of profits which derives its motivation to do so rather than pure Altruism and Philanthropy. Which if you ever have seen the stellar HBO show Silicon Valley then you know some good laughs are made from this 'making the world a better place' meme, tackling the blind hubris that is the real Silicon Valley satirically. You should watch it – it is really good.

Google has invested in high-broadband optic fibre internet for locations such as Kansas City, Austin, Salt Lake City, and Atlanta.* Google does not invest in this out of pure Altruism and high-speed internet for the peoples. They do this because the more people that use the internet, the more people use Google, and the more data Google have, and the more adclicks Google can sell. In the same vein one of Google's Moon-Shot ideas is to bring internet to third-world countries. Ideas like floating balloons beaming broadband down to the surface has been circulating for a while.* Again, this is not because Google has a good heart and knows that internet access raises educational levels and as a result raises the GDP of that country. It is because Google monetarily benefits from such an operation.

But in the digital ointment lies a fly. In the short and midterm this seems like a noble and admirable business practise. Businesses get their Return on Investment and the country benefits socially, and the world environmentally. But there is as reason governmental institutions of that country adopts this role. Businesses, especially the ones that have to be large enough to carry out these massive investments, are stock exchange traded multinational enterprises. Corporations who have a fiduciary responsibility of growth and financial gains for their shareholders, not the citizens of the third world countries. If businesses start to own and operate what has historically been the responsibility of governments, like roads, schools, police, and the fire department. Then what is to stop these businesses to over time profit on these very services?

For example, releasing a new product-offering of different fire accident coverage plans, like broadband plans. Making full coverage more expensive than semi-coverage. So the consumer, not citizen, that cannot afford full coverage, maybe does not see the fire truck arrive in time, before their home is burned down. This is obviously put on edge, but there is a very real futuristic scenario that the business practise of Creating Shared Value will lead to the dystopian fictions we see in movies like Blade Runner, if not heavily regulated and legally controlled.

So the businesses must never own these invested public

goods and only carry these operations out for long-term profit making, without enacting obvious control. An important point, which has to be iron cladded in a legally binding document, with very real consequences if not followed. Although maybe this is naïve, since if over time private enterprises owns more and more social goods and governmental institutions themselves, then they would also own the police to enforce the law, the judiciary system to enact the law, and the prisons to send you, ergo themselves, if breaking this contract; if breaking the law.

5 THE ELEPHANT IN YOUR ROOM MADE OF YOUR DATA

In order to tackle privacy, we have to make clear about the central questions that we have to start with. Since as it is now, privacy is given by default to whomever you are in a democratic liberal-humanistic nation – it is perceived as a human right. You have a right for privacy through the philosophies that has shaped the society you live in, ultimately begun from religious beginnings. But if Thomas Jefferson, Immanuel Kant, and Robert Nozick is not enough, although we will cover this in a bit, then we can find some connections within nature.

In the same context that dogs hide animal bones, a squirrel burying its stash of nuts for later use and other squirrels playing James Bond in getting these stashes of nut-goodies. It seems like that a right to privacy is existent within nature. If we link it with human nature, we can see that in the development of our children, then they need a safe and private environment to grow up in to make mistakes, to then learn from.

Both nature and nurture make this privacy notion originate as one of the most central aspects of being human. Everything you think, your consciousness, what is going on inside of your mind is private by default and has primed your behaviour into treasuring your privacy as a right. This means that we instinctively value our privacy, just like that if you ever meet a person that claims to read your thoughts, and can prove it through a theatre performance going viral, we would instantly imprison that person. And yet, we more times than not give our privacy away freely. So, what is happening? What is this Privacy Paradox, previously covered? So far we only have been descriptive of the value embedded in privacy. We have not covered the facts, or the means to which we keep our privacy – the normative.

The United States in the 1890s was one of the first to protect normatively a person's private right to bodily harm and property, the second one can be seen as privacy.* Tim Urban from the brilliant 'Wait but Why' blog in his latest, best and longest series 'The Story of Us'*, describes this effectively as a larger green circle around each person, and a closer red circle around each person as well. The green circle is indicative of one's rights in the public sphere, that can be foregone if stepping into another's private property.

Essentially meaning that if you are a visitor in someone's own home you willingly forego your green-circle rights for some delightful company and oven-baked potatoes. While the red circle is your inalienable right that cannot, under no circumstances, be impeded upon without consequences.

If another's green circle collides with another's green circle in public, it is fine, although complicated. It is when another's green circle collides with another's inner red circle that the government has to step in and protect that persons red circle. John Stuart Mill says this in a more eloquent manner as, "the only purpose for which power can be rightfully exercised over any member of a civilized community, against his will, is to prevent harm to others."* He branded this neatly as the Harm Principle. Originally going against what the norm was across the pond of excessive control over people through namely monarchies.

The problem is that this removal of one's green circle, within a private property, is the case both for Aunt May's private domicile. But also, for sites like Facebook and YouTube. Since these are considered private platforms with rights, it's their own house. In a figurative sense, we need to figure out if our private right of our data is within the green circle or within the red circle. If it should be handled by our own conscious judgment of which it is done in the vast majority of cases, or within the red circle of which no compromising, of any kind, of private data is allowed.

Whatever happens inside your own four walls, individual company, or person, as long as you do not harm anybody, meant in a both literal and figurative sense, means your privacy is your own. Mind you that this privacy can be overruled by a common collective fiction we have call the judicial system. If we have enough reasonable doubt and supporting evidence that you are indeed hurting someone within your private domain, then this can be foregone to be investigated. Even removing your red-circle rights by the government if proven to be guilty. Everyone knows this, this is nothing new.

But since this is a central aspect of our society and almost everyone agrees on this, then what is the issue with the invasion of privacy we feel today by the big technology platforms – again, what are the specific questions?

Privacy can be removed for the common good. The complication arrives as to figure out where it starts and where it ends. The recently terminated Patriot Act in the United States made it possible for the government to spy on you and everyone else to prevent terrorism, or at least that was how it was stated. Terrorism is a real thing; it brings harm for the common good. But is it justifiable to remove the right of privacy for all, for this potential threat of the few? Many would say no. Side note, it has later been found out that the Patriot Act and subsequent spying did not stop any terrorist actions, following allegations that it was all to spy and control the American people. I will not go into this in detail, since it has little to do with the platforms, but as a rule of thumb, the more lovely sounding an Act is the worse it usually also is. So be aware of the Save The Puppies Act, as Edward Snowden joked about in the Joe Rogan Experience podcast.* There is some truth to it, since naming of governmental slogans and, well, names are usually defused of any real meaning or actions. Like how can you be against "Hope" or "Making America Great Again"? You really can't, but if you really look at them, they don't say much, they don't have much substance.

Okay, back to privacy. Here is another example, today we have the ability to monitor people's energy and utility usage. Not only in the public sphere through online-enabled Smart Cities, but in people's own homes as well. Meaning that by probing for behavioural data more efficient energy and utility usage can be instigated for the good of everyone. This then follows the question; is an individual's privacy rights less important than the right for all to have a liveable environment?

Obviously, this is set as an extreme to further understanding, but the questions through this seems, therefore, to be on who is doing the data probing? How is the data handled? Is the data probing generalised or specific to one individual? What are the intentions behind the acquired data? And do we fully understand what our data is being used for, when we are giving it up?

Let us dig in.

With the advent of new technologies, more intrusive methods of privacy-impeding is available. Just to name a few, we have seen rental car companies track rented cars through GPS to see if their renters were speeding, resulting in large fines if doing so.* Biometric data, such as fingerprints and iris scanning in your eyes, is being used to unlock phones and other personal electronical devices and are stored in companies' data bases. Additionally, an FBI surveillance program named Carnivore appears to sample information from multiple internet users, not only suspects, to build cases.*

The first is a private company putting in a contingency plan for protecting their rented-out property, lessening speeding, but also profiting from this – an ethical grey area. The second, are private companies storing biometric individual data that are normally preserved for public entities. Enabling these companies to use this biometric data to more effectively track people of where they are, for potential commercial use – a fully ethical bad area, if found out if that was the case. The third, a public entity exercising data intrusion to make our common environment better – to some extend an ethical grey area. But most would agree that this is overreaching of power from a public entity. Since the data probing is generalised rather than specific towards potential perpetrators. The main point is that data privacy ethics has to be talked about on a one-to-one basis to figure out a generalised doctrine to regulate when to start and when to stop this data probing.

Since this is a book about the platform business model, specifically towards the large technology platforms, we need to first outline the problem with these. The central issue between the ethical breaking of data privacy with the platform business model is that intrusive data acquisition and usage is central to the success and growth of the platform business model itself. Essentially pitting up the growth of business incentives against moral usage of data and data acquisition. If you then want to change unethical usage of People Data – Your Data – then change the Dataminer business model; look at the disease rather than the symptoms. But we are getting ahead of ourselves.

Before we go into the actual economics and business reasons why data is so tightly tied to the platform business model success, we have to zoom out and see it more generally, with the platform category of the Dataminer. The influential Immanuel Kant came up with a principle he called the Humanity Formulation. Kant argued that in order for humanity to be moral in our actions we should not make people act for us as a means to get to an end.* This is formulated a bit confusingly, so here is an example, put on the edge, to further understanding.

You really like candy. That coloured chemistry is just your thing. You walk past a candy store, unfortunately, going out of business, "I guess people buy their candy online", you thought. In your thought process you see a sign saying, "everything is for free – since we go out of business *sad-emoji*". Your face lights up, because oh chuca-lai-lai do you want that candy. But as you reach for the door, it is jammed and by no means can be opened.

Panic sets in and you feverously dart around to find nice, old grandpa George. In your decrepit moral behaviour, you grab George as a means to get into the candy store. You throw him through the window and are now in the candy shop munching on the coloured dopamine pieces, with a severely hurt grandpa George on the floor, lightly hulking, in pain.

Businesses are here to make money. It is their fiduciary responsibility, but also, if the business did not make money there would be no business. In the same way the Dataminer platform makes its money on data and the selling of it. Its end is money, and the Dataminer are using their consumers, you and me, as means to get it. A practise that would go against moral behaviour of what Immanuel Kant came up with as the Humanity Formulation.

The growth reasons why People Data, as it is known, is so linked with the platform business model are:*

People's data provide exclusive insights in the behaviour of consumers and unique insights into market trends. These insights directly aid the product development and market strategies the Platform-owner uses to generate growth. If done successfully this can create exclusions for competing entities that have limited, or no access to this data. As a result, this distorts competition when the data hoarders keep their data under lock and key. A familiar conduct and incentive to keep this as non-transparent as possible. The complication is that it creates an unfair advantage. Smaller Platform-owners, with smaller consumer sizes, does not aggerate enough data in order to receive these unique insights and cannot grow effectively compared to the data hoarders. An aspect which the platforms where consumers tend to only use one platform, like Google, is a large issue. Because the consumer's behaviour of only being on one platform aids this data hoarding strategy and keeps out of competitors to break into this platform market.

In a roundabout way this also ties into the problem of economies of scale when it comes to People Data aggregation and usage. There is a strong collation between how much data a Platform-owner has aggregated, and the effectiveness of the growth strategies employed. Which incentivises Platform-owners to use more and more intrusive data acquisition methods and goes against the privacy standards and laws many countries operate under. Essentially the more data you have, the stronger your business governance can be and when you connect this with businesses fiduciary shareholder incentive of growth and profit, you have a problem.

This leads us to a more ambiguous utilisation of People Data: the tailoring of services and products towards the individual consumer. This in marketing lingo is known as personalised marketing and is with the amount of data that a Platform-owner can aggregate on an individual consumer. This Platform-owner can within reason tailor whatever service or product this Platform-owner offers to your individual liking.

For example, Netflix can through your watching patterns and what you liked, suggest exactly what you would like to watch. In this way it maximises your enjoyment of the platform and maximises time-spent on Netflix and lessens the possibility of you ending your subscription, going to the Game of Thrones realm. This is in general considered to be a positive thing. But what if Netflix purchases your data from Facebook? So, your

Instagram behaviour and WhatsApp messages are being gawked at to track what your larger interests are, who you are underneath your entertainment choices? Or how about purchasing data points from Google - peering into your emails on Gmail to see what you are talking about with your friends and family, to figure out what theme their next Netflix Original should have? All these instances could be the case, but generally with the Pay-upper category a steady and reliant cash flow is set up so no need to manipulate you is an incentive all that much. The scene gets much grimmer when we look at the Dataminer category, like Facebook, Twitter, TikTok, and Google.

Today the sophistication of data fidelity and acquisition has reached such heights that it can be linked with your mood. In digital marketing this is called 'Mood Targeting' and is through your typing speed, what you search for, how you phrase sentences, which apps you use, at what times you use them - the Dataminer platform can gage your emotional state. There are even technologies out there that can through the selfie camera on your smartphone take a picture of your face and analyse with unsettling accuracy how your emotional state really is.* Although this is, as far as we know, not in use, only a possibility with scientific findings, prototypes and patents.

But if put into use this mood-information is then sent to advertising agencies that can use this to target you specific products that would sell better when you are in a content mood versus a sad one – Tranquilene, the American depressive medicine, would be very keen on this data and list of consumers. But for the general advertising agency this can be utilised to sell you different adverts that has either a sad or happy theme to it, so you connect more unconsciously to it. The Dataminer platforms, thereby those that are monetarily free of charge, but not emotionally or attention-wise free of charge, can then set a premium price point for this information, due its uniqueness and effectiveness for the advertisers, to increase profit margins and please their fiduciary responsibility. In other words, you are the means to get to the end.

The New York Times, ESPN, and USA Today all have publicly stated that they currently use Mood Targeting, using self-learning algorithms to predict what mood you are in.* Although more details are unknown about this and it is hard to find, so to what extent, if this is individualised to profile single customers, or generalised to target the group, or if they frame their articles in a certain way based on this to get you to read more, is again, unknown.

But it does not stop there – the real-life Black Mirror episode gradually comes into view the more you look into this. The big bad Dataminer, Facebook, decided to carry a social experiment that mirrors that of Alex Huxley's 'Brave New World'. Facebook wondered if moods would be contagious and more specifically, contagious online. They randomly chose almost seven-hundred-thousand test subjects to subjugate posts related to a certain mood. One could solely see happy posts, one hopeful ones, and one with only depressing ones. The result was that mood contagion is a thing; test subjects predominantly posted more of what they were subjected to.* The happy ones posted more happy posts, and the angry ones, posted more angry posts. Effectively heightening the Echo Chamber effect even higher, which we have talked about earlier, and has become part of the common tongue. As Alex Huxley's 'Brave New Word' said, "Consider the horse – they considered it."

Now, whatever the intentions, the fact that test subjects were picked at random without knowledge about them poses the bigger ethical problem. Because what if a test subject, or in non-scientific language, you or your child or your mother, was depressive and prone to suicide. Would this experiment have pushed them over the edge to commit suicide, due to the predominantly depressive exposure on Facebook?*

One last, potential, example before we go into surveillance. Is that Google through their search algorithms, structures the internet and makes the immense pool of our collective knowledge manageable. But it also highlights in many ways who you are, your deeper interests, political leaning, and your personality. Here businesses would be keen on purchasing this People Data, this You Data, both for commercial intentions, but also, for people that could be potential employees. Maybe Google themselves do this for their hiring process internally, we don't know. Realising that you actually are not the person right for the job, because you during your uni-years where critical of big technology's influence on the world, or that they discovered that certain personality types does not mesh with this role, so you get discounted not on your skillset, but on your personality or teen-mistakes.

Data probing creates a surveillance effect of a change in our behaviour from what we originally would have had. But it isn't that simple, because you cannot just replace your personality, replace your behaviour, you instead hide it behind a fake veil. "To know and not to know, to be conscious of complete truthfulness while telling carefully constructed lies, to hold simultaneously two opinions which cancelled out, knowing them to be contradictory and believing in both of them, to use logic against logic, to repudiate morality while laying claim to it…"* as it was said in the quintessential 'Nineteen Eighty-Four' by George Orwell. The main point is that it decreases our notion of freedom, which is directly against one of the most fundamental values of liberal-humanistic nations: our autonomy, our individuality. To illustrate this, we have to ask the late French philosopher Michel Foucault and psychoanalyst Jacques-Alain Miller of their thoughts on the panopticon prison design, related to coercing your behaviour.

Foucault and Miller got note of a prison design that had been circulating within prison architects for a while. A design that promoted a more efficient, hands-off controlling of prisoners through architectural ingenuity. Rather than using torture and dank dungeons, exerting more outward control and punishment, modern democratic societies needed a more subversive way of making sure that bad actors did not ruin it for all. They looked at the panopticon prison design and drew a parallel between the design's notion of coercive surveillance to inadvertently change people's behaviour.*

If someone believes they are being watched, they will change their behaviour, no matter if they are actually being watched or not. So that you can get a sense of the panopticon prison design it would be built as a cylinder with prison cells on the inner side of this cylindrical design with transparent cell-doors. In the middle of this prison, there would be a 360-degree guard tower with tinted windows. The prisoners cannot see anyone inside this guard tower, but always, at all times, has the possibility that a guard is looking directly at them. This would coerce the prisoners to change their behaviour no matter if they actually are being spied on or not.

In a way this panopticon idea can be translated into our general modern democratic world. With the advent of more surveillance and data probing measures from private companies, not just public ones, will coerce people's behaviour and limit their freedom – essentially change people's actions but done commercially, not in line with civil obedience, in line with buying more stuff we don't need.

The famous book 'Surveillance Capitalism' by Shoshana Zuboff* links the surveillance and gathering of information of people to knowledge about the market to gain strategically the upper hand. The more People Data, your data, a business entity aggregates, the more effective strategies can be employed to gain growth. But it connects deeper into what our Capitalistic system is build up on. The best way to describe this is to travel far in the past, of the exploratory motivations carried out, mostly, by European powers from the 15th to the 19th century. It is the notion of accepting and be comfortable with not knowing.

Admittance of ignorance is no novel realisation for capitalists and businesses alike. The large trading companies of the early modern age did not only ship goods on their trading vessels or soldiers to protect them against other competitive trading companies or wealthsmitten pirates. They also had botanists, geologists, anthropologists, archaeologists, biologists, cartographers, and so on. They knew that understanding the world and the new places they found could lead to better strategies to generate yet more cash flows and trade control. But it all centred around the admittance of ignorance, of that we do not know – so if we do not know it, we go out and seek answers. This was the front and centre of the Age of the Enlightenment, of rationalism.*

Today we use statistics and market research for this very admittance of ignorance. Business Analysts are employed every day to crack unique insights into business consumer habits and larger economic trends. The difference today is the advent of data aggregation in mass and self-learning algorithms to aid them.

The market in the old definitions of capitalism, from Adam Smiths to Friedrich Hayek, contended that knowledge is power. That the market is always ambiguous and intrinsically unknowable. No one can understand the inner workings of the market and since no one can understand and predict the market, competition will always be a levelled playing field. Surveillance Capitalism, together with advanced self-learning algorithms, are starting to gain insights into the market that has never been seen before. Adding this with the massive amounts of data aggregated. Means that if the notion of what makes capitalism fair is that everyone is equal under the market's unpredictability, means that if businesses in the form of platforms have overcome this, then they have successfully thwarted capitalism and gained too much market power and influence.

As Cameron Marlow, back in 2012, head of the Data Science Team inside of Facebook reflected on the wealth of insights able to be achieved, "this is the first time the world has seen this scale and quality of data about human communication … For the first time, we have a microscope that … lets us examine social behaviour at a very fine level that we've never been able to see before."* And from the words of Eric Schmidt from Google himself, back in 2010 said, "You give us more information about you, about your friends, and we can improve the quality of our searches. We don't need you to type at all. We know where you are. We know where you've been. We can more or less know what you are thinking about."*

Alarming statements since we are about a decade away from these comments. But let us dwell a bit on the 'you give us more information about you and your friends, to create better products for you' part.

It is said that we do not care about our privacy any longer. That we agree on being spied on in our usage of, especially, the Dataminer platforms. We knowingly share our behaviour and our data to use this service free of charge. While in the act of sharing, we know that we collectively make these platforms better for all, but equally that they can tailor the platform to our own benefit, our specific needs. This is directly the case with Google's services, linking it with news Google think you find pressing, connecting your Google Calendar with your Google mail and in extension every other service online you use your Gmail to connect to. A few points support this notion. For example, look at the data-sharing we carry out today at a conscious level. If we put our sharing mentality from today and put them back in the Cold War ridden 1950's, scoffs and collective disapproving would be surrounded by you.

Additionally, people knew back when Facebook was 'The Facebook' about Social Media prior - they just had to take a gander at MySpace. What was innovative with 'The Facebook', was that rather than using your handle "BikeFan4Real" or "LoverOfCakes69" – was that you used your real name, your actual age, and your deepest interests – because your network did the same, taking real life into ones and zeroes. In this way, the evidence has showed that we have changed our behaviour and viewpoint on privacy and data. That platforms are just capitalising and following the times and does what is considered fine.

A counterargument to this is that back in 2007, the 'The Facebook' days, people did not know how much about data probing that would occur here in 2021. People signing up with their name, age, and interests did not sign up for being spied on of where they are at all times, all their search histories, their constant emotional state, and so on and so forth. A slow, creeping slippery slope has occurred, so people did not notice or flag it – remember the boiled frog metaphor from earlier? People do not know what they are signing up for and is within data privacy circles known as the previously mentioned Privacy Paradox, since people do this anyways or are not looking into this, but values their privacy, nonetheless.

To see this from the opposite point of view. Google and others have stated that the services they provide are aided by the data you are sharing. The reason why Google Maps are better than Apple Maps is because of this data sharing element – making it more personal and effective. The reason why Google Search is better than Bing and Yahoo! is because of their tracking of what you have searched for in the past. That your future search results are personally modified. So, would we be willing to sacrifice worse digital services and products for higher privacy?

Additionally, we all know that a business is here to make money. We know a trade-off is present when we use YouTube to watch videos. We know that in order for the service to be free, we watch ads. This is complicit in the agreement of watching YouTube videos to begin with. Is this the same with data sharing as well?

Maybe people know that if you are using Google's services, you know that these services are for free – but it actually is never free. To take the Google Maps example again. We know that there are no traditional ads on Google Maps, as of the moment of writing this book, and we know that a business is here to make money – so how are they making money then? Through data sharing and your people data. Shouldn't we then know that sharing data is complicit in this usage contract of it being free? Would you be willing to pay a monthly fee to Google for all their services, to effectively and completely remove all of their advertising and probing for your data, while also accepting a worse service? Maybe this is too late – maybe the cat is so far out the bag, that its playing with its scratching tree in a living room, in another house, in another country. But the international court of justice could force Google to offer up such a Payupper solution of monthly payments. Changing Google's business model from a Dataminer to a Frankensteiner, with the implementation of the Payupper. Making it up to the individual to choose the level of data probing they want.

In April 1930 the BBC newscaster, at the scheduled timeslot for news, went on to briefly say "there are no news" and shifted to some relaxing tunes.* Today the BBC runs on data and in its place for mindful tunes, has around-the-clock no-news news broadcasts. Oscar Wilde said it perfectly as, "… Accurate and prosaic details of the doings of people of absolutely no interest whatsoever."* Even when news eventually strike, the only "good" news, is the tragic and disheartening news.

Maybe the perspective on your own private data should by default be owned by you. That you reside and choose what and to whom your data is shared. In a way this is already being inadvertently chosen, with the services you choose to use. Although transparency has definitely not been the technology platforms first priority. For example, if you have a Facebook account, and log on or even enter a different website, if that website has that little Facebook logo at the top. Then that website, through online cookies – through that Facebook logo, sends back to Facebook that you have been on that website. Effectively prompting Facebook to advance their profile about you to sell to advertisers. Even in some instances if you have deleted your Facebook profile – Facebook still saves the profile about you internally.

This 'ownership of your data' notion links with individualism and private property laws. The idea goes that you are your own entrepreneur of your own data and you can sell this data willingly for a fee at a global People Data stock exchange, like gold or crude oil. Or directly to whatever business you decide to use, using your data is your currency. The reason why this solution is starting to gain traction is that People Data exceeded the value of gold back in 2017.* So, you have gold bars in your pocket that you do not know that you have – this solution brings this out in the light and make you have private ownership over your own private data gold bars.

The upside of this solution is that it connects well with the dominant "ism" the majority of our nations are run by today, liberal humanism, with a splash of neo-classical economics in there for good measure. It connects well with individualism because it turns the individual to reside and decide over their own data – a concept known as subjectivism within the ethical schools of thought.

6 AN ENLIGHTENED AND INFORMED PUBLIC

The French political philosopher Jean-Jacques Rousseau was not a fan of Democracy.* He thought that this system, echoing Plato, would denigrate into Tyranny. This through an oscillating cycle of Aristocracy, whether it be ladies or lords, samurais or jarls, or career politicians; to Timocracy of coastal elites and cocaine-ed Wall Street bankers; to then Oligarchy of widening the circle of monied trust to the intellectuals and from the twopercenters to the five-percenters; to then our good old, Democracy; but from mass rule it denigrates into Tyranny, aided by opportunism; rinse, repeat.*

The reason why Rousseau thought of this, is because he thought the central element for a Democracy to work is to have an enlightened and informed public. A core belief which he thought is only possible with a miniscule part of the public – not the larger populace. The farmer, the manager, the engineer, and the nurse does not want to be a representative of government, while also having a family, full-time work and hobbies on the side. Likewise, in order for a public to be informed and enlightened, means a sensible information network has to be there to achieve these things alongside a well-developed education system. The solution was therefore to set up people who would adopt these roles, since no individuals wants to delve into the complexities of all things government; from economics to infrastructure to police to foreign policy. So the general populace elects those very individuals. Rousseau rebottled this by saying it does not defeat the larger problem of that it still requires an informed and enlightened public to then vote for the right people. While the people that then run for office would inherently be first idealists, to then over time turn into opportunists, treating government as a career.

What we see with the advent of the media platforms of today is a disruption of the old media networks and essentially the sense-making machine of our world – the fourth estate. New media like Facebook, Instagram, TikTok, and Twitter, is making money by maximising time spent on their platform. They employ echo chamber systems to slot you in a group that you agree with on issues concerning public matters. This is done to entice you to stay on their platform for monetary reasons and even now able to manipulate the larger mood of a people the size of countries emotional state as mentioned earlier.

While this is happening, the traditional once powerful media channels are losing viewership and readership fast. This makes them irrational - trying to hold on as best they can. They take a cue from the echo chamber system and only report the news that their last remaining loyal viewers and readers would like, to keep them on their platform. Essentially what we see now is the dying breadth of the old media and the rise of the new. But the consequences of all this is that we lose the sense-making system essential to having an informed and enlightened public. See old media, the fourth estate, biased and self-censoring as they may be, trumpeted by Noam Chomsky, still exposed you to different topics and unified a country through a unified message – even though it was propagandised. Now with a decentralised sense-making system, like new media of today, and an educational system more times than not failing, we are lost in what knowledge is, what truth is, and how to acquire it. We have an ontological problem today, and most people do not have the time or energy to fact check or develop their own advanced view of topics that other people takes PhDs in, like economics, foreign policy, sociology, international relations, political science and so on. We are at the mercy of what the fourth estate told us, who to vote for, which people best for our own wellbeing. This Rousseau did not believe in, so he was against Democracy. But it is difficult to come up with a viable alternative. Other than putting up checks and balances to be elected into office; one, you have to have X amount of experience within the field you are elected in, or Y you have to be thoroughly psychological evaluated, if not passed, no office for you, and to put motivations in order, to align career-politicians goals with the goals of the people, the salary and pension paid could be a commission-based system like sales people today in companies, to get paid of how well your nation is doing. If the nation is doing poorly, then your paycheck is poor.

In a short, one-liner sentence; with the advent of the Dataminer media platform, Democracy has been destabilised from within because of a less enlightened and informed public.

The consequences can in most instances be seen on the effects of our children. Kids when they grow up with a new technology, will adapt themselves to this new technology. Which in effect will change the development of their brain and behaviour accordingly. Studies have naturally been done and we see worrying results. The previously referenced Adam Alter book spoke to a number of psychologists who deal with addictions from platforms such as the Social Media ones – the Dataminer ones. Here they said that Social Media had completely reshaped the brain of the kids. Into not being able to distinguish between interpersonal relationships physically as opposed to digitally. The psychologists reflect that the scenarios the kids go through in their therapy sessions of drama between their friends or complications with their girl- or boyfriend are laid out as it transpired in real-time, face-toface. Where in reality it all happened over text. One of the psychologists even said, "this person doesn't differentiate various modes of communication the way I do ... the result is a landscape filled with disconnection and addiction."*

A study was made with kids participating in a camping trip. Before and after this trip the kids had to take an empathy and behavioural test called DANVA2, short for Diagnostic Analysis of Nonverbal Behaviour. You basically get shown a bunch of photographs, audio and video clips, and you have to determine what mood the people shown are in. Are Mona Lisa happy because she is smiling or bored because of her eyes? The DANVA2 contains multiple of these emotive people, where it progressively gets more and more difficult to tell the exact mood. The camping trip the kids were on had banned all use of electronical devices and put an emphasis on being physically with each other. They were tested before and after this trip and it was found that the kids where about thirteen percent better at telling people's emotions and emotional states compared to before and after this trip. A result that can lead one to think that the physical isolation and digital interaction tears on the ability of interpersonal skills. It makes sense, you never see people in person, you never read their body language, if only interacting with people over electronical devices. An alarming conclusion since this only was based on a week away from the Dataminer platforms like Facebook, Twitter, TikTok, Snapchat, and Instagram.* Although many other factors can also be found. For one it is speculated that being in nature boosts temporarily one's cognitive abilities. But I digress.

To make matters worse, we have the absorbent mass of the internet, with an abundant collective of information both true and false. The internet is both amazing in that we all have become all-knowing gods. But also problematic in that we do not know what information shown are true or false. Whatever belief you hold, whatever collective truth you live by, you can find supporting statements online for just about anything. We struggle today with determining how we know what we know to be true. And the internet heightens this due to this ambiguity. I even wrote a whole chapter about this in my philosophy thought experiments book called, "5 Thought Experiments to Change Your Perspective".* But enough of the shameless self-promotion.

McLuhan once said, "societies have always been shaped more by the nature of the media by which men communicate than by the content of the communication."*

Attention is seen as a zero-sum game. If you go out in nature and listen, you will notice a barrage of sounds and sensory impressions. Schools of birds chirping away shouting, "this is my territory! This is my tree!", leaves rustling profusely in conjunction with wind-sweeping blows. If you are a botanist, they would be able to never stop babbling about the intricacies and fascinations of what is around you in the moss, swamp water, the skittering beetles between your feet, and so on. And yet we find immense peace, meditation and tranquillity in nature and the sounds of it.

Impressions are, therefore, not the issue. It is attempts at your attention that are the issue. As is written in the New Philosopher magazine about attention and fake news by Nicholas Carr, "in this world of overfilled inboxes, push notifications and digital billboards – is an overload of attempted communication: a cacophony of efforts to stake a claim on our attention."*

The platform business model, and more tellingly, the Dataminer, that are engineered to generate profits through advertising and the selling of People Data comes from engagement and attention given to their platform. This attention aim has taken over the sense-making machine of our nations and eroded us to be less enlightened and less informed. Cracking democracy from within and dividing us further apart like never before. The method of which to change this is to change the business model central to the Dataminer category within the platform business model itself. You have to look at the disease, not the symptom. The problem is that you are used as a means to gain a profitable end. While also regulating the People Data ownership from businesses to themselves. Managing and using the businesses own data and engagement consciously in the capitalistic surveillance market machine. The ethics of the platform seems to be to regulate the Datamining category and how the data is being utilised – not the overall platforms themselves. But to be the devil's advocate, is here a viewpoint that platforms, like Google, rightly can defend themselves on.

Google orders and filters information based on the bias of you - how they have profiled you. They do this to give you what they believe is the most useful information for you at the moment in time when you Google something.

Information is never neutral. There is always a choice being made, a bias to show, subjectivity to be based on. If you Google "Hong Kong", a fully neutral information result would just be random facts shown about Hong Kong; the population size, their economy, the square footage, and so on. Essentially the Wikipedia information box on the right side of the screen.

But this is rarely what you look for when Googling a topic like Hong Kong. If you are a historian, should it instead be the historical and political strife in its history with Britain's Imperialism, like the Opium Wars? Or maybe you have searched in previous enquiries that you are interested in geopolitical topics, or that you have family currently living in Hong Kong. Should it then be the current political and identity complications in Hong Kong, with being shifted from part of the UK Commonwealth back to China, Chinese rules and the Chinese judicial system? Or let us say you are a tourist and needs something to do. You heard about a famous festival, but you do not remember its name. You Google 'Hong Kong' and it shows you the Hong Kong Arts Festival, whether COVID cancelled it, and what dates it would be live.

Information-filtration is extremely complicated and there is an argument to be made that in Google's profiling you, based on your data, does this to show you the best answers to your Google enquiries, which are the most ethical and noble choice Google can do. Otherwise, you always just get a standardised Wikipedia box of information in every search.

But if this act of bias is based on a far-reaching

surveillance-arm stretching all around you from only one corporate entity's hands. If this is unethical, is the answer then to break it up or to close it down? Again, Google would say no, obviously. But not just because there would be no Google, but because of the severer consequences this would have globally. A person today consciously choosing not to use Google or any other search engine, would be held back in life. For example, a person refusing to use Google will struggle if having to do their taxes and the tax rules just changed. Or let's say that, that person wanted to start a business in the state of Florida, what then are the rules and requirements to do so? Can that person figure that out without using Google? Also, services like YouTube have significantly increased knowledge regarding niche topics, raising awareness of topics previously unknown.

By force-closing Google we would halt our progress as a people and the wonder both our ancestors from hunter-gatherer times and the agricultural revolution would see as God-like powers. Having access to an organised, bias or not, database of all our collective human knowledge at the ready, at the ends of our fingertips – we have all become Odin, Seshat, Orunmila, Wenchang Wang, Apollo, Saraswati, I can keep going. But most of us does not know what to do with all this information – our sense-making is challenged. A lot of us are contend with being just receivers and repeaters of information, ignoring the legitimacy of this information or the impact thereof. We in a way see ourselves loosing what is central to us, our moral compass - gradually becoming cybernetic organisms, part you, part Google.

Paul Romer from the New York Times therefore suggested not going the legislative route, but a digital advertising sales tax route. Maybe the answer to all of this is not to bring down the hammer of justice, but impose taxes on the Dataminer model to provoke the transition into a Frankensteiner, essentially a Payupper model. Since with the advent of a sales tax on digital advertising revenue will make the potential earnings tilt the favour towards subscription revenue, rather than data mining. While to target the problem of the platform business model being designed towards monopolising, this tax could be a progressive tax. Increasing in percentage based on the size of the digital advertising revenue itself.

Although it is a limited view on a possible solution, since it does not consider the transfer pricing practise that multinational enterprises carry out to lessen their tax payments today. Or the heavy lobbying that will be pushing for politicians to not instigate this digital advertising revenue tax. But this solution, as an alternative to legislative action, is admirable.

The short story by famous science fiction author Ken Liu, has an perfect quote in his short story 'Perfect Match' to exemplify this, "Churchill said that we shape our buildings, and afterward our buildings shape us. We made machines to help us think, and now the machines think for us."*

But this is not the end. We know the dangers of the platform; we know the shivers it gives us when we are spied on. The answer is to do something about it, we have the unique position of self-reflection – we are partially wise animals, wise sapiens. We will look back at our era and see that we had the beginnings of something amazing, our wisdom and morale just needs some adjusting. Let us follow this advice and get up from our seats, stop being a spectator and a repeater, and get into the damn ring.

Thank you so much for reading and listening to this book – it is an honour that I do not take lightly!

If you want to reach out to me, ask me a question or just engage in lovely conversation, not necessarily about this, rather than me writing a bunch of lettering symbols to then beam them into your eyes or ears.

You can write to me at jhpii.writer@outlook.com

Again,   thank   you.

SOURCES AND ACKNOWLEDGEMENTS

Alter, A. (2017). Irresistible: The Rise of Addictive Technology and the Business of Keeping Us Hooked. Retrieved from https://www.amazon.co.uk/Irresistible-AddictiveTechnology-Business-Keeping/dp/1594206643

Andrés Latapí Agudelo, M., Jóhannsdóttir, L., & Davídsdóttir, B. (2019). A literature review of the history and evolution of corporate social responsibility. International Journal of Corporate Social Responsibility.

Bagchi, A. K. (2005). Perilous Passage: Mankind and the Global Ascendancy of Capital. Rowman & Littlefield Publishers.

Barth, S., & de Jong, M. D. T. (2017). The privacy paradox – Investigating discrepancies between expressed privacy concerns and actual online behavior – A systematic literature review. Telematics and Informatics, 34(7).

Bown, S. R. (2010). Merchant Kings: When Companies

Ruled the World, 1600--1900. Thomas Dunne Books.

Business Casual. (2018). When The Dutch Ruled The World: The Rise & Fall of the Dutch East India Company. Retrieved from YouTube website: https://www.youtube.com/watch?v=ewCs5CF5HEg

Carr, N. G. (2017). Information Overload. NewPhilosopher - Fake News.

Chomsky, N., & Marr, A. (1996). Noam Chomsky on Propaganda - The Big Idea - Interview with Andrew Marr. Retrieved from YouTube - BBC website: https://www.youtube.com/watch?v=GjENnyQupow

CrashCourse. (2015). Capitalism and the Dutch East India Company: Crash Course World History 229. Retrieved from YouTube website: https://www.youtube.com/watch?v=zPIhMJGWiM8

de los Reyes, G., Scholz, M., & Smith, N. C. (2017). Beyond the "Win-Win." California Management Review, 59(2), 142–167. https://doi.org/10.1177/0008125617695286

Deci, E. L., & Ryan, R. M. (2000). Self-Determination Theory and the Facilitation of Intrinsic Motivation, Social Development, and Well-Being. American Psychologist, 55(1), 68–78. https://doi.org/10.1002/jsfa.2740050407

Desjardins, J. (2017). The Most Valuable Companies of All-Time. Retrieved from Visual Capitalist website: https://www.visualcapitalist.com/most-valuable-companies-all-time/

Dommer, S. L., & Swaminathan, V. (2013). Explaining the Endowment Effect through Ownership: The Role of Identity, Gender, and Self-Threat. Journal of Consumer Research, 39(5), 1034–1050.
https://doi.org/10.1086/666737

Economics Explained. (2020). The Economics of the Dutch East India Company. Retrieved from YouTube website:
https://www.youtube.com/watch?v=hjVFwqM7xuo

European Commission. (2017). Antitrust: Commission fines Google €2.42 billion for abusing dominance as search engine by giving illegal advantage to own comparison shopping service. Retrieved from European Commission website:
https://ec.europa.eu/commission/presscorner/detail/en/IP_17_1784

European Commission. (2018). Antitrust: Commission fines Google €4.34 billion for illegal practices regarding Android mobile devices to strengthen dominance of Google's search engine. Retrieved from European Commission website:
https://ec.europa.eu/commission/presscorner/detail/en/IP_18_4581

European Commission. (2019). Antitrust: Commission fines Google €1.49 billion for abusive practices in online advertising. Retrieved from European Commission website:
https://ec.europa.eu/commission/presscorner/detail/en/IP_19_1770

European Commission. (2020). Speech by Executive Vice-President Margrethe Vestager: Building trust in technology. Retrieved from European Commission

website:
https://ec.europa.eu/commission/commissioners/2019-2024/vestager/announcements/speech-executive-vice-president-margrethe-vestagerbuilding-trust-technology_en

Federal Trade Commission. (2021). The Antitrust Laws.
Retrieved from Federal Trade Commission website:
https://www.ftc.gov/tips-advice/competition-guidance/guideantitrust-laws/antitrust-laws

Foucault, M. (2020). Discipline and Punish: The Birth of
the Prison. Penguin Classics; 1st edition.

Friedman, M. (1970). A Friedman doctrine -- The Social
Responsibility Of Business Is to Increase Its Profits. The
New York Times.

GillPress. (2021). Big Data Quotes of the Week. Retrieved
from Whats The Big Data website:
https://whatsthebigdata.com/2012/06/16/big-data-quotes-of-the-week-9/

Hagiu, A., & Wright, J. (2015). Multi-Sided Platforms. In
SSRN Electronic Journal.
https://doi.org/10.2139/ssrn.955584 T4 - From
Microfoundations to Design and Expansion Strategies M4
– Citavi

Herman, E. S., & Chomsky, N. (1995). Manufacturing
Consent: The Political Economy of the Mass Media.
Vintage.

Hern, A. (2018). 'Never get high on your own supply' –
why social media bosses don't use social media. Retrieved
from The Guardian website:
https://www.theguardian.com/media/2018/jan/23/never-get-high-on-your-own-supplywhy-social-media-bosses-

dont-use-social-media

Inoue, Y. (2019). Winner-Takes-All or Co-Evolution among Platform Ecosystems: A Look at the Competitive and Symbiotic Actions of Complementors. Sustainability, 11(3).

Jackson, R. H. (1937). The Philosophy of Big Business. Before the American Political Science Association.

Kahneman, D. (2012). Thinking, Fast and Slow.

Katz, B. M. L., & Shapiro, C. (1985). American Economic Association Network Externalities, Competition, and Compatibility. 75(3).

Katz, M. L. (2019). Multisided Platforms, Big Data, and a Little Antitrust Policy. Review of Industrial Organization.

Katz, M. L., & Shapiro, C. (1986). Technology Adoption in the Presence of Network Externalities. 94(4).

Kramer, A. D. I., Guillory, J. E., & Hancock, J. T. (2014). Experimental evidence of massivescale emotional contagion through social networks. PNAS, 111(24).

Kuran, T., & Sunstein, C. R. (2007). Availability Cascades and Risk Regulation. Stanford Law Review, 51(4), 683. https://doi.org/10.2307/1229439

Latif Dahir, A. (2020). A Bird? A Plane? No, It's a Google Balloon Beaming the Internet. The New York Times. Retrieved from https://www.nytimes.com/2020/07/07/world/africa/google-loon-balloon-kenya.html

Lefebvre, H. (1991). The Production of Space (1st ed.).

Retrieved from https://www.amazon.co.uk/Production-Space-Henri-Lefebvre/dp/0631181776

Lewandowski, M. (2016). Designing the Business Models for Circular Economy — Towards the Conceptual Framework. Sustainability, 43(8), 1–28. https://doi.org/10.3390/su8010043

Lewis, T. (2019). AI can read your emotions. Should it? Retrieved from The Guardian website: https://www.theguardian.com/technology/2019/aug/17/emotion-ai-artificialintelligence-mood-realeyes-amazon-facebook-emotient

Liu, J., Wang, H., Hui, C., & Lee, C. (2012). Psychological Ownership: How Having Control Matters. Journal of Management Studies.

Liu, K. (2016). Perfect Match. In The Paper Menagerie and Other Stories (p. 464). Gallery / Saga Press; Reprint edition.

Loth, V. C. (1995). Armed Incidents and Unpaid Bills: Anglo-Dutch Rivalry in the Banda Islands in the Seventeenth Century. Modern Asian Studies, 29(4), 705–740.

Lozano, R. (2013). Are companies planning their organisational changes for corporate sustainability? An analysis of three case studies on resistance to change and their strategies to overcome it. Corporate Social Responsibility and Environmental Management. https://doi.org/10.1002/csr.1290

McGarvey, R. (2015). Is Your Rental Car Company Spying on You and Your Driving? Here's How They Do It. Retrieved from The Street website:

https://www.thestreet.com/personal-finance/insurance/car-insurance/is-your-rental-carcompany-spying-on-you-and-your-driving-heres-how-they-do-it-13089306

McKinsey Center for Business and Environment. (2016). The circular economy:Moving from theoryto practice.

McLuhan, M. (1967). The medium is the massage. Penguin.

Mill, J. S. (2016). On Liberty. CreateSpace Independent Publishing Platform.

Moore, A. D., & Martin, S. (2020). Privacy, transparency, and the prisoner's dilemma. Ethics and Information Technolog, 13.

Moses, L. (2018). Project Feels: How USA Today, ESPN and The New York Times are targeting ads to mood. Retrieved from Digiday website: https://digiday.com/media/project-feels-usa-today-espn-new-york-times-targeting-adsmood/

National Center For Education Statistics. (2020). Characteristics of Public School Teachers. Retrieved from The Condition for Education website: https://nces.ed.gov/programs/coe/indicator_clr.asp

NewPhilosopher. (2017). Extra! Read all about it! NewPhilosopher - Fake News.

Noah Harari, Y. (2014). Sapiens: A Brief History of Humankind. Retrieved from https://www.amazon.co.uk/Sapiens-Humankind-Yuval-Noah-Harari/dp/1846558239

Orwell, G. (2013). Nineteen Eighty-Four. Penguin Modern Classics.

Pierce, J. L., Kostova, T. and Dirks, K. T. (2003). The State of Psychological Ownership: Integrating and Extending a Century of Research. 7(1).

Pii, J. H. (2021a). 5 Thought Experiments To Change Your Perspective. Retrieved from https://www.amazon.co.uk/Thought-Experiments-Change-Your-Perspectiveebook/dp/B08XZPWX4J/ref=sr_1_2?dchild =1&keywords=5+thought&qid=1615383240 &sr=8-2

Pii, J. H. (2021b). A Beginners Guide to the Platform Business Model: The business model that Amazon, Google, Apple, Microsoft, and Facebook share and that you are missing out on. Retrieved from https://www.amazon.co.uk/Beginners-Guide-Platform-BusinessModelebook/dp/B08Y79R6C6/ref=sr_1_3?dchil d=1&keywords=Platform+Business+Model&qi d=1615231716&s=digital-text&sr=1-3

Piketty, T., & Goldhammer, A. (2017). Capital in the Twenty-First Century. Belknap Press: An Imprint of Harvard University Press.

Porter, M. E., & Kramer, M. R. (2011). Creating Shared Value: How to reinvent Capitalism - and unleash a wave of innovation and growth. Harvard Buisness Review - The Big Idea.

Rodriguez, A. (2018). YouTube's recommendations drive 70% of what we watch. Retrieved from Quartz website: https://qz.com/1178125/youtubes-recommendations-drive-70-ofwhat-we-watch/

Rogan, J., & Harris, T. (2020). Joe Rogan Experience #1558 - Tristan Harris. Retrieved from YouTube website: https://www.youtube.com/watch?v=OaTKaHKCAFg
Rogan, J., & Snowden, E. (2019). Joe Rogan Experience #1368 - Edward Snowden. Retrieved from YouTube website: https://www.youtube.com/watch?v=efs3QRr8LWw

Rousseau, J.-J. (2018). The Social Contract (Abridged E). Digireads.com Publishing.

Selinger, E., & Hartzog, W. (2015). Facebook's emotional contagion study and the ethical problem of co-opted identity in mediated environments where users lack control. 12(1).

Smith, A. (2014). The Wealth of Nations. CreateSpace Independent Publishing Platform.

Stanford Encyclopedia of Philosophy. (2016). Kant's Moral Philosophy. Retrieved from Stanford Encyclopedia of Philosophy website: https://plato.stanford.edu/entries/kantmoral/#HumFor

Stanford Encyclopedia of Philosophy. (2018). Mill's Moral and Political Philosophy. Retrieved from Stanford Encyclopedia of Philosophy website: https://plato.stanford.edu/entries/mill-moral-political/

Statista. (2021). College enrollment in the United States from 1965 to 2018 and projections up to 2029 for public and private colleges. Retrieved from https://www.statista.com/statistics/183995/us-college-enrollment-and-projections-inpublic-and-private-institutions/

The Economist Leaders. (2017). The world's most

valuable resource is no longer oil, but data. Retrieved from The Economist website: https://www.economist.com/leaders/2017/05/06/the-worlds-most-valuable-resource-isno-longer-oil-but-data

The United States Department of Justice. (2020). Justice Department Sues Monopolist Google For Violating Antitrust Laws. Retrieved from The United States Department of Justice website: https://www.justice.gov/opa/pr/justice-department-sues-monopolistgoogle-violating-antitrust-la

Tsotsis, A. (2010). Eric Schmidt: "We Know Where You Are, We Know What You Like." Retrieved from Techcrunch website: https://techcrunch.com/2010/09/07/eric-schmidtifa/

Urban, T. (2019). The Enlightenment Kid. Retrieved from Wait But Why website: https://waitbutwhy.com/2019/09/enlightenment-kids.html

Wikipedia. (2021a). Carnivore (software). Retrieved from Wikipedia website: https://en.wikipedia.org/wiki/Carnivore_(software)

Wikipedia. (2021b). Dutch East India Company. Retrieved from Wikipedia website: https://en.wikipedia.org/wiki/Dutch_East_India_Company

Wikipedia. (2021c). Google Fiber. Retrieved from Wikipedia website: https://en.wikipedia.org/wiki/Google_Fiber

Wikipedia. (2021d). New Holland (Australia). Retrieved from

https://en.wikipedia.org/wiki/New_Holland_(Australia)

Wikipedia. (2021e). Plato's five regimes. Retrieved from Wikipedia website: https://en.wikipedia.org/wiki/Plato%27s_five_regimes

Wilde, O. (2019). The Critic as Artist. ekphrasis.

Wilson, N. S. (1965). Freedom of Contract and Adhesion Contracts. The International and Comparative Law Quarterly, 14(1).

Zuboff, S. (2015). Big other: Surveillance capitalism and the prospects of an information civilization. Journal of Information Technology, 30(1), 75–89. https://doi.org/10.1057/jit.2015.5

ABOUT THE AUTHOR

When J.H. Pii was 5 years old his brother found him a bamboo stick from the yard. His eyes lit up and began to erratically wave it around like a madman. He was subconsciously searching for a spot to run amok and eventually ended up on a battered brown leather couch in his newly renovated to be open-plan, open-plan 1950s childhood living room. He called his stick "Bird Stick", because he waved it in such a way as to create illusory wings from this speedy effect, with his (usually right) hand as the bird body. Why are we talking about Bird Sticks? I hear you profusely proclaim as you gave this piece of text a change to go down and read all "About The Author". Because J.H. Pii had for years and years trained himself in narrative construction: how characters develop, intricate plot designs, deep worlds, twists and turns, even voice acting! Yes, J.H. Pii acted out loud. It was a hoot to be a spectator to.

As an adult J.H. Pii is a Polymath.
He deep dives into these obscure topics within History, New Technologies, Business, and Philosophy. But he comes out on the other end with, usually, something interesting to write about.
But see, his be all, end all, is to make this writing as engaging and entertaining as possible. Discovering new topics and insights by no means have to be watching paint dry. So J.H. Pii uses his years of prowess into narrative structure to write about these heady topics that in equal parts entertain you and enlightens you – making you curious.

All in all, so we all wish to hand-fly - just like J.H. Pii does.